JONAH

Fifteen Days with the Runaway Prophet

TOM FRENCH

JONAH: FIFTEEN DAYS WITH THE RUNAWAY PROPHET

Copyright © 2021 Tom French
All rights reserved

ISBN 978-0-6483041-6-6
Ebook ISBN 978-0-6483041-7-3

First published 2021 by Frendrussi Press
Melbourne, VIC, Australia

No parts of this publication may be reproduced, stored in a retrieval system, or transmitted in any form or by any means, electronic, mechanical, photocopying, recording, or otherwise, without the prior written permission of the copyright owner.

This book is sold subject to the condition that it shall not, by way of trade or otherwise, be lent, resold, hired out, or otherwise circulated without the publisher's prior consent in any form of binding or cover other than that in which it is published and without a similar condition including this condition being imposed on the subsequent purchaser. Under no circumstances may any part of this book be photocopied for resale.

All scripture quotations, unless otherwise indicated, are taken from the Holy Bible, New International Version®, NIV®. Copyright ©1973, 1978, 1984, 2011 by Biblica, Inc.™ Used by permission of Zondervan. All rights reserved worldwide. www.zondervan.com. The 'NIV' and 'New International Version' are trademarks registered in the United States Patent and Trademark Office by Biblica, Inc.™

The website addresses recommended throughout this book are offered as a resource to you. These websites are not intended in any way to be or imply an endorsement on the part of the author, nor does he vouch for their content.

Cover illustration by Matt Baker
Paperback edition printed by IngramSpark

For Sebastian and Hugo –

May you always know that you are loved,
on earth and in heaven.
Pop wouldn't be Pop without you.

Contents

Acknowledgements	6
Introduction to Pop's Devotions	9
Introduction to Jonah	14
Day One: Surprise! *Jonah 1:1*	22
Day Two: The Call *Jonah 1:1–3a*	26
Day Three: Getting Down *Jonah 1:3–5*	30
Day Four: Bad Reputation *Jonah 1:6–10*	34
Day Five: The Goodness of Pagans *Jonah 1:11–16*	39
Day Six: Fish Time *Jonah 1:17*	43
Day Seven: Rescue Song *Jonah 2:1–4*	47
Day Eight: Prophet in a Foxhole *Jonah 2:5–7*	51
Day Nine: The Idolater *Jonah 2:8–9*	55
Day Ten: Fish Vomit *Jonah 2:10*	59
Day Eleven: Words of Power *Jonah 3:1–5*	63

Day Twelve: Hear, Feel, Do *Jonah 3:6–10*	67
Day Thirteen: Family Values *Jonah 4:1–4*	71
Day Fourteen: Ordered Love *Jonah 4:5–9*	76
Day Fifteen: The Last Question *Jonah 4:10–11*	80
Afterword	84
Bibliography	90
Also by Tom French	92
About the Author	94

Acknowledgements

This book came about because mid-2020 Covid-19 pandemic, while I was stuck running youth group online, I was trying to think of a way to help my youth group engage with the Bible. As we couldn't see each other in person every week, I thought maybe if I made some devotions and posted them online, my youth would watch them, listen to them, or read them. At the time of writing the videos are on YouTube, the podcast is up, and the emails of the first draft of these devotions have been sent to a bunch of people – but I'm not sure if anyone in my youth group has consumed them. I hope so, but I'm not holding my breath. I'm going to give all of them a copy of this book in print, so maybe they'll at least read this bit, because it's about them. Hey there, Inner North Youth Group! Whether you actually read any of this book or not, I'm very thankful that I get to be your youth minister. Thanks for putting up with my dumb jokes, for indulging my failed game ideas, and for giving me a reason to keep teaching the Bible. I love getting to see God at work in each of your lives. And I love that you keep teaching me how to teach the Bible to people like you.

I'm also very thankful for my father, John (also known as Pop) who has shown me what it means to be a man who seeks to hear from God through his word daily. I hope my devotion is as faithful as Pop's devotion.

My thanks go to all those people who did read, listen to, and watch the first draft of these devotions. I appreciate your feedback and encouragement. Thanks especially to Nathan, the only person outside my family to fill out the survey telling me what he thought of the book. Who knew that online surveys were so unpopular? I guess we all got burned by Cambridge Analytica.

Jo Stockdale, my editor, once again, has made a messy book as good as one of my books can be. I'm always impressed by how she whips these things into shape. If I ever get to visit the UK, I'll buy you a thank you pie or something. I'm not sure what food says 'thank you' in British.

I also very much appreciate Gina Denholm's majestic proofreading. Though she works with many of Australia's theological heavyweights, she treats my work like it's just as important (which is weird, but good).

Matt Baker has done the excellent cover artwork. I haven't seen it yet because I'm writing this before the cover is done, but if I haven't deleted this paragraph you can be sure I love it.

These last twelve or so months have been pretty wild, so I'm very thankful for the support of Merri Creek Anglican, the INYG youth leaders, Graham Stanton, the youth ministry Co-Op, and all those others who have kept me going during 2020.

Chris Morphew, we made that podcast! Maybe we'll get the book written? Also, thanks for sharing your Jonah chapel talks with me. They were super!

As always, I'm so thankful to and for my loving and supportive family across the border and the world. Jane, John, Jo, Hannah, Victor, Sebastian, Hugo, Grandpa, Valentina, and Oscar. What a team! I love you all.

Layla! Welcome to the world, you squirmy old thing. I love you and I love having you around.

Emily is my constant champion, my excellent wife, and my love. I'd still be pottering about with my first book if it wasn't for you believing in me.

Finally, God – Father, Son, and Holy Spirit – it's all for and because of you. To God be the glory.

Introduction to Pop's Devotions

I love reading my Bible in the morning. It makes me feel great! I feel like a super-Christian for doing the thing that people have been telling me I should do all my life – reading my Bible. Unfortunately, however much like a super-Christian I may feel, I can often read huge chunks of the Bible and feel like I've not taken anything in. I may have understood all the words along the way, but I couldn't tell you much about what I read. I could, however, tell you about whatever insignificant thing I was daydreaming about as my eyes glanced at each of the words in the passage.

If the goal of reading the Bible is to tick a box so you can say you're a good Christian, then it's not too hard for me to do that. But if the goal of reading the Bible is to pay attention to what it's saying and hear from God as he speaks though it, then I have to admit that I struggle.

So I like to get help when I read the Bible. I often use books or apps to give me some other people's reflections on a passage because it helps me pay attention to what

I'm reading. Sometimes they have excellent, inspiring, and challenging things to say about the passage, and I get insights I would never have thought about on my own. Sometimes I think what they say is almost entirely wrong. But even disagreeing with someone makes me engage with the Bible and figure out why I think what they're saying is wrong.

People often ask me, 'Do you know any Bible devotions for youth?' I have one book that I always recommend and then I'm done.[1] This doesn't mean there aren't any good ones out there. I just haven't found them. So instead of searching every available teenage devotional to try to find the good ones, I thought I'd write some myself. I can't guarantee the devotions are good, but I can guarantee that they're here, in this book, and I wrote them. I'll let you be the judge of their quality.

WHY ARE THEY CALLED 'POP'S DEVOTIONS'?

I didn't really want to call my series of devotions *Daily Wisdom from Pastor Tom French*, partly because no one calls me Pastor Tom French, but mostly because I don't enjoy naming things after myself.

Unlike me, my father, John French, is very good at spending time with God. In fact, he has done it almost every day since 1964. Growing up, I'd see him in the

---

1. If you're interested, that one book is *Best News Ever: Your 100-Day Guide to the Gospel of Mark* (Epsom: The Good Book Company, 2019) by my mate Chris Morphew. It's especially good if you're in year eight or below, but I read it and found it helpful and I'm at least three years out of high school.

mornings reading his Bible and spending time in prayer. Occasionally, I'd wake up at 5am to the sound of him singing hymns alone during his morning devotions. He showed me what it's like to spend time with God every day, so I thought, 'Who better to name my devotions after than my father?' His actual name isn't Pop, but his grandkids call him Pop – hence, Pop's Devotions!

HOW DOES THIS BOOK WORK?

I assume you could probably figure out how to read the devotions yourself, but if you're the kind of person who loves reading all the instructions, here are some ideas on how to use this book.

Each devotion is broken up into a few parts.

First, you get a passage of the Bible to read. So grab your Bible and read it. You can read it in a paper Bible, on an app, on a website, or listen to it read aloud. You may have noticed that there are lots of different translations of the Bible. I recommend the NIV, but there are plenty of good options out there. You will see that you repeat this reading over multiple days. This is because each day has a focus verse or verses, but these are only short, so to make sure you don't forget the context of what we're thinking about, I give you a longer passage to read. I promise reading the same passage a few days in a row will help you understand the book a lot better, and it won't take too long.

Before you read the Bible, it's a good idea to pray and ask that you would hear God as he speaks to you through his Word.

Next, I give you some things to consider. I have tried to give you some background information on the passage, and some ways it might make an impact in your life.

Remember, these are my thoughts on the passage. So if you read them and they're helpful, great! If you don't like them, that's okay – they aren't the Bible. I have tried to get things right, but I can make mistakes. So if your pastor or someone else who knows a lot about the Bible disagrees with me, that's okay too. It's an opportunity for you to do some further reading and praying and see what you think.

Following my thoughts, I give you a question to reflect on. It's important to consider how the Bible impacts you, so try to spend some time reflecting on the question.

Next, I suggest something you could do. I do this because the Bible should not just give us interesting things to think about; it should make a practical difference to how we live. If, after reading the passage, you find God is challenging you to do something else, fantastic! Do that! God's instructions are much more important than mine.

Finally, I give you a prayer to pray. Each prayer is just one or two sentences long, so use it as a springboard to help you begin your time of prayer with God. Tell God whatever you want. Tell him what you love about him, what you're thankful for, what you're sorry about, and what you'd love to see him do. He wants to hear from you, and I promise, once you start

Introduction to Pop's Devotions

praying, you'll start seeing his answers all throughout your life. This is the amazing thing about our heavenly Father who is excited to be in relationship with us.

GIVE YOURSELF A BREAK

My last piece of advice is this: give yourself a break. There are fifteen days of devotions in this book. If you're having a good time reading them every day, wonderful! However, if you're feeling the pressure to read them every day, or you miss a day or two (or more), no worries. There's nothing wrong with having a day off, spending time reading something else, or just spending time in prayer and reflection. Feel free to take seventeen days, or twenty days, or thirty days to get through this book. God still loves you, even on the days you don't read your Bible. And he definitely doesn't love you more if you force yourself to do devotions every day. If you're spending more time with God because of Pop's Devotions (or any other devotions) than you normally would, then count it as a win.

Now, let me tell you a little about the book of the Bible we're about to study.

Introduction to Jonah

When did you first come across Jonah? If you've spent any time hanging out with Christians as a kid, there's a good chance you met Jonah when someone told you the story of the runaway prophet who got swallowed by a whale. Perhaps at some stage you've also read the story or seen the movie of Pinocchio. If so, you may have images in your head of someone sitting in the belly of a whale and you're not sure which is the biblical prophet and which is the puppet who wanted to be a real boy. (Which one is the story with the donkeys?)

The problem with the book of Jonah is that we have reduced it to being only about the fish that swallowed Jonah. Of course, the bit about the fish is a key moment, but as you'll see, the fish is only mentioned in three verses in the entire book. The book of Jonah is much more about a not-very-good prophet learning about God's mercy for all people.

Here is some information about the book of Jonah that may be helpful to think about as you read it.

WHAT IS JONAH ABOUT?

If the book of Jonah isn't about the fish, what is it about?

The book sits in the Bible among a bunch of books called the minor prophets. These prophets are minor not because they're less important than the major ones but because the books are shorter. When you read the book of Jonah, you may be struck by how different it is to all the surrounding books. All the others are full of powerful and poetic oracles describing the sins of Israel and the nearby nations, and promises of God's judgement and restoration. Jonah, however, is a story. There are characters, dialogue, and miraculous goings-on, all while the main character finds himself on an adventure. This isn't your average minor prophet.

However, beneath the story, we can see that the writer of Jonah clearly has a lesson to teach. As Jonah learns about God's mercy for people he doesn't like, we, the readers, learn about God's mercy for people whom we may not like. As Jonah is challenged about God's compassion towards all his creatures (including humans and livestock), we too are challenged to 'allow' God to have compassion on all his creatures today. Obviously, we don't give God permission to *do* anything – he does what he wants. But we can, like Jonah, be offended by God's all-encompassing love. Jonah's challenge becomes ours too: to let God be God, and invite him to align our hearts with his.

While we don't know exactly when the book of Jonah was written, it was clearly designed to help its first readers (or hearers, as it would have been read aloud) to consider how they should respond to their enemies. If the book was written around the time of Jonah (perhaps even by Jonah himself), then the Assyrians (where Nineveh was the capital city) were bearing down on the people of the northern kingdom of Israel (Jonah's people). Eventually, in 721 BC, they would invade and take the people of Israel into captivity. The book of Jonah would have been a tough book to read as an Israelite facing that future.

If the book of Jonah was written later, after the invasion of Israel in 721 BC and after the southern kingdom of Judah was taken into captivity by the Babylonians in 586 BC, then the challenge of the book would have held no less of a sting. The captured people of Judah, who may have begun returning to their ravaged homeland, would have been forced to consider how they would like God to treat their enemies who had caused them so much strife.

The book of Jonah seems like a fun little story, but it packs a lot of punch. As we read it today, we equally must face the challenge of its lessons for us. Like the Israelites of Jonah's time, we live in a divided world where we can hope for, and perhaps even revel in, the destruction of those we don't like. As we watch people get cancelled and publicly shamed, as we jump on the bandwagon of public judgement, God has questions to ask us, just as he questioned Jonah. I'm sure as we get stuck into the book of Jonah we'll be challenged to consider who deserves God's grace. Are we willing to align our hearts with God's character, or are we swayed by the character of the culture we inhabit?

IS IT A TRUE STORY?

Beware: controversy ahead!

One discussion that has been going on for some time is whether the book of Jonah is really a true story. I know this might seem like an offensive question. We may think, if the book of Jonah is in the Bible, then it must be a true story. However, perhaps we shouldn't be so fast to jump to conclusions. Just because we read a story in the Bible doesn't mean it actually happened. For instance, is Jesus' parable of the Lost Son in Luke 15:11–31 a true story? The story is true in the sense that it tells us the truth about God's love for sinners, but the story itself is fictional – it's a parable Jesus made up to help teach us about God's love. Is there a chance that Jonah could be a similar genre of story?

We know Jonah was a real person because we read about him in 2 Kings 14:25. But that doesn't mean that some writer wasn't inspired by the Holy Spirit and the real-life Jonah to write a fictional story about him to teach the people of Israel something true about God. It's a bit like when real people turn up in fictional movies. Bill Murray is in the story of *Zombieland* as Bill Murray, but as far as I know, Bill Murray has never been a zombie – that's just a fictionalised version of the real person.

So it's possible Jonah the real-life prophet was picked by the writer of Jonah the book to be the hero of a fictional parable.

Now, before you get upset that I'm doubting the Bible is real (or trying to entice you to doubt the Bible), let me say this: I wholeheartedly believe that the Bible is the inspired word of God. I believe that Jesus physically rose from the dead, that he is God, and that he literally performed all the miracles described in the Gospels. I also believe the stories in Acts and the Old Testament history books are real. I have no problem with believing in the Bible or its miraculous stories; I'm just suggesting that Jonah may not be one of them.

I have a few reasons for thinking that the book may be a work of fiction. My first reason is because it reads like fiction. If you read biblical history books like 1 and 2 Samuel and 1 and 2 Kings, you find books full of geopolitical and interrelational complexity. Compare them to Jonah and there is nothing incidental in the story; every element serves to drive the story forward. Also, the behaviour of each character in the story fits the pattern of upending traditional expectations: the bad guys are good, and the good guy isn't that good. All this suggests that the story may be the construction of someone's (Holy Spirt-led) imagination.

My second reason is because there aren't any historical records of the whole of Nineveh repenting, which we read about in Jonah 3. It's not even reported in other books of the Old Testament. You would think that if an entire capital city chose to stop torturing and killing people, it would appear somewhere in the history books. As I mentioned above, the Assyrians invaded Israel in 721 BC. If they had converted to belief in Israel's God, as seems to happen in Jonah 3, you would think they would at least give the invasion a second thought. But there is barely any indication in biblical history that the Assyrians even paused to consider whether asserting dominance over Israel was the right thing to do.

My last reason is because there are some things in the book of Jonah that seem to be inaccurate or exaggerated. For instance, the leader of Nineveh is referred to as the 'king of Nineveh' (Jonah 3:6) but that was never a title in real life. There was a king of Assyria, but no king of Nineveh. Also, the writer of the book of Jonah says that 'Nineveh was a very large city; it took three days to go through it' (Jonah 3:3). That is an absurdly large city! You could walk from one side of Melbourne (where I live) to the other in less than a day (according to Google Maps), and Melbourne has a population over forty times the stated population of Nineveh (Jonah 4:11).

'Hold on,' you might think. 'Jesus tells us that Jonah was a true story.' It's true that Jesus refers to Jonah in Matthew 12:38–41:

> Then some of the Pharisees and teachers of the law said to him, 'Teacher, we want to see a sign from you.' He answered, 'A wicked and adulterous generation asks for a sign! But none will be given it except the sign of the prophet Jonah. For as Jonah was three days and three nights in the belly of a huge fish, so the Son of Man will be three days and three nights in the heart of the earth. The men of Nineveh will stand up at the judgment with this generation and condemn it; for they

repented at the preaching of Jonah, and now
something greater than Jonah is here.'

However, Jesus' reference to Jonah doesn't necessarily mean that he believed that the story of Jonah happened. I may say to you, 'As the Avengers fought to protect New York from aliens, I will fight to protect my house from ants' but, hopefully, you wouldn't think that I really believed that the Avengers fought to protect New York. The ants may be real, but the Avengers are not.

The point of Jesus' discussion here is not to prove, or disprove, the historical accuracy of the book of Jonah, but to rebuke the Pharisees and the teachers of the law for their demand for a sign. He contrasts the men of Nineveh, who were willing to repent at the preaching of Jonah, with his opponents, who were unwilling to repent even at Jesus the greater prophet's much greater preaching. For Jesus' point to work, the story of Jonah does not need to have really happened, it just needs to be a story in the collective consciousness of his opponents.

All that said, I'm probably only about 50.5 per cent convinced that the book of Jonah is a fictional story. That part where Jesus refers to the men of Nineveh certainly makes more sense if the book of Jonah is a real story. If I wrote this introduction tomorrow, maybe I'd be 50.5 per cent sure that the story really happened, just as it's recorded. Smarter people than me think it's a true story, not to mention that for most of history people have read it as a true account, and I wouldn't want to suggest that I know more than them. If the book turned out to be telling a true story, I would be very happy (how could you not be excited to know that a dude really did get swallowed and vomited by a whale?). I don't think the guts of the book change that much if the events of the story did or didn't actually happen. The challenge of the book – to consider how our hearts align with God's – is still the same. The heart of God and his preference for grace remains unchanged. So whether you think the story of Jonah really happened or not is not the main issue. Don't get distracted from the challenge for us in this tale about a runaway prophet and his compassionate and gracious God.

DAY ONE

Surprise!

FOCUS VERSE: JONAH 1:1

READ: Jonah 1:1–6

SOME THINGS TO CONSIDER:

I once went to the movies to see an animated kids' film with a friend. As we were settling in with our popcorn and Coke, a very real-looking shot of an American city street came up on the screen, accompanied by some ominous music. I was fairly sure this was not the film we'd bought tickets to see. I soon figured out this was not a light-hearted film for children, but a slasher flick that was guaranteed to be full of teenagers getting stabbed by some unknown killer. If the cinema didn't put the right film on soon, all the surrounding families were going to have a

Day One: Surprise!

surprisingly different film-going experience from the one they were expecting.

You may know Jonah as a story for kids because there's a guy who spends a few days living a fish, but this is probably not the story you're going to find. While Jonah isn't a surprise story about people getting stabbed by an unknown killer, what you'll discover, whether you were reading the book thousands of years ago when it was first written or you're reading it today, is that the story of Jonah is not quite what you thought it would be.[2]

The first thing we read in the book is, 'The word of the Lord came to…' Just as the words 'Once upon a time…' or 'Mr. and Mrs. Dursley of number four, Privet Drive…' let you know exactly what kind of story you're reading, these first words of Jonah tell us what we're about to read is a book of prophecy. Prophecy is when God's thoughts and desires are made known to his people through someone who speaks them. In the Bible there is a bunch of books of prophecy, books like Isaiah, Jeremiah, Obadiah, and the mildly amusingly named Habbakuk. Normally, we'd expect a lot of talk of God's people's sin, and how God is going to restore them, but in this book we're in for a treat because instead we get, well, the story of Jonah. This is a story where a prophet runs away from God, some pagan sailors are better theologians than the professional prophet, a fish swallows then vomits up a man, a city of killers turn to God, some cows repent, and

---

2. If you are looking for stories in the Bible of people getting stabbed, there are plenty of those. There isn't quite a slasher flick book of the Bible where attractive Israelite High Schoolers get murdered by a killer in an ancient hockey mask, but you can't have everything.

a worm makes a grown man's life so terrible he wants to die. Like I was saying, this is not the book of prophecy the ancient Israelite readers would have been expecting, and if this is the first time you've come across Jonah, at least since you were a kid, this is probably not the story you were expecting either.

None of this is a mistake, not like the accidental slasher movie we almost watched. Sometimes God speaks to us in surprising ways to reveal unexpected things, but this is the God who saved the world by dying for it, so God's surprisingness shouldn't really be surprising at all. We might think we've got everything with God buttoned down, figured out, and neatly sorted, but a book like Jonah has the startling power to turn everything upside down if we let it.

Are you willing to discover things about God and yourself that you might not have been expecting? It's not too late to turn back and find something safer to read. Just don't make the mistake of running from what God has to say to you, because you can be sure you won't get far.

SOMETHING TO REFLECT ON:

How do you feel about God having surprising (and maybe uncomfortable) things to say to you through Jonah? Nervous? Excited? Sceptical? Bored? Spend some time reflecting how you feel about the journey through Jonah that lies ahead.

SOMETHING TO DO:

Keep an eye out today for the things that surprise you. When you do, remind yourself of the surprising things God has already done for you and what he has taught you.

A PRAYER TO PRAY:

God, you can work in some unexpected ways. Help me be open to the ways you may want to work in me as you speak to me through the story of Jonah. Thank you that you have saved me in the most surprising way, when you sent your Son Jesus into the world to die and rise to new life for us.

DAY TWO

The Call

FOCUS VERSES: JONAH 1:1-3A

READ: Jonah 1:1–6

SOME THINGS TO CONSIDER:
When you get a call on your phone, how likely are you to answer? If I don't know why someone is calling, whether I know them or not, I often let the call go to voicemail. If someone wants a long chat, I want to be ready. If someone wants to ask me for something, I want to be ready. Unfortunately for you and me, and Jonah, there is one call that can't go to voicemail.

It's God's. You probably figured that out, but you know, just in case it wasn't obvious, you can't let God's call go to voicemail because God doesn't use a phone. Also,

Day Two: The Call

you shouldn't ignore God. But if Jonah and God both had phones, I bet Jonah would have just let this one ring. And if God messaged, he would have left him on read.

Seeing as we're now on day two of our two weeks with Jonah, it might be worth getting to know this prophet who actively avoided God's call. He is the principal character in this book after all. You may think Jonah only appears in the book of Jonah, but you'd be wrong. Jonah has a crossover appearance in 2 Kings. King Jeroboam II, who was then the king of Israel and a pretty evil king, had some military victories winning territory back off his enemies and 'restored the boundaries of Israel'. This glorious victory happened 'in accordance with the word of the Lord, the God of Israel, spoken through his servant Jonah son of Amittai, the prophet from Gath Hepher' (2 Kings 14:25).

Jonah was the good guy prophet for the bad guy king. Imagine getting that mission from God: 'Go tell the king that he's going to have a military victory that restores honour to his nation.' Yes, sir! What a great assignment. Jonah was probably celebrated in the court of the king for his excellent prophecies. And I bet he looked back fondly on those times, when he was hanging with the rich, famous, and powerful, going to all the best parties, eating great food, and wearing fancy clothes, because he had the good word of the Lord.

Then we come to the beginning of the book of Jonah, and God is giving him another message to deliver. This time he wasn't to speak to anyone in Israel, but to preach against the city of Nineveh because 'its wickedness has come up before [God]' (Jonah 1:1). What was this wickedness?

Nineveh was the capital city of Assyria, one of the great powers of Jonah's time. The Assyrians were famous for their cruelty. The kings of Assyria would boast about the terrible things they did to their enemies. Things like (and if you're eating your breakfast right now you might want to skip this bit) tearing people's limbs off while they were still alive, burning teenagers alive, and stretching people out with ropes so they could be skinned, also while alive. They would cut off people's heads, put the heads on a pole, and make their friends carry the pole around. These were not good people.

So you can imagine how Jonah felt when he was asked to go preach against them. We aren't told yet why Jonah ran away, but on the surface it seems pretty clear. Those Ninevites were not the sorts of people you'd want to mess with. This was a very different assignment from being asked to tell a king he was going to win some amazing battles. Preaching against the Ninevites would be like rocking up to a Mexican cartel and trying to run a drug education seminar. It was probably not going to go too well.

What would you have done? I probably would have done the same as Jonah. I would like to keep all my limbs and skin, thank you very much.

So here's the rub. Have you ever longed to hear the voice of God? Have you longed to know God's plan for your life? But what if you discover that God is calling you to do something that you don't want to do? What if your plan is for a comfortable life, and he wants you to be uncomfortable for the sake of his kingdom? It's not outside the realm of possibility. Jesus, whom we follow, died on the cross. His disciples were called to share the news of God's salvation and were persecuted and killed for it. You may want to hear from God, but you may not want to hear what he has to say. Jonah might seem like a bit of an idiot, but don't judge him too quickly – you may be more like Jonah than you think.

SOMETHING TO REFLECT ON:
How would you have responded to God's command to Jonah? What does that tell you about how you might respond to God's uncomfortable commands to you today?

SOMETHING TO DO:
Is there something you know God has asked you to do but you're avoiding doing it? Perhaps there is a relationship you need to mend, an enemy you need to reach out to, someone you need to seek forgiveness from, a sin you need to turn from, or a friend you need to share Jesus with. There is no better day than today to do what God has asked of you.

A PRAYER TO PRAY:
Heavenly Father, thank you that even though I sometimes resist your commands, you still love me. Please forgive me for the times I have resisted you. Help me to hear your voice clearly and, by your Spirit, obey you faithfully.

DAY THREE

Getting Down

FOCUS VERSES: JONAH 1:3-5

READ: Jonah 1:1–6

SOME THINGS TO CONSIDER:

Every year in the United States, approximately one hundred firefighters are arrested for arson.[3] These are people who should be fighting fires, and instead they're out there starting them. Jonah, the runaway prophet, like an arsonist firefighter, did the exact opposite of what he was supposed to do.

In verse two, when God tells Jonah to 'go to the great city of Nineveh', some Bible translations leave out

---

3. *Report on the Firefighter Arson Problem: Context, Considerations, and Best Practices* – https://www.nvfc.org/wp-content/uploads/2016/02/FF_Arson_Report_FINAL.pdf

a little bit of the original text, which has God saying, 'Get up!' But what did Jonah do instead? He went in the opposite direction. He went down to Joppa to catch a boat, he went down into the boat, and he lay down and fell into a deep sleep. God said 'Get up', but Jonah went down. Jonah was doing the exact opposite of what God asked him.

Nineveh was east of Israel, where modern-day Mosul is in Iraq. Tarshish, Jonah's intended destination, was about as far west as you could go in the opposite direction. People don't know exactly where it was, but have a look at the handy map I've drawn, showing you where scholars think Tarshish may have been:

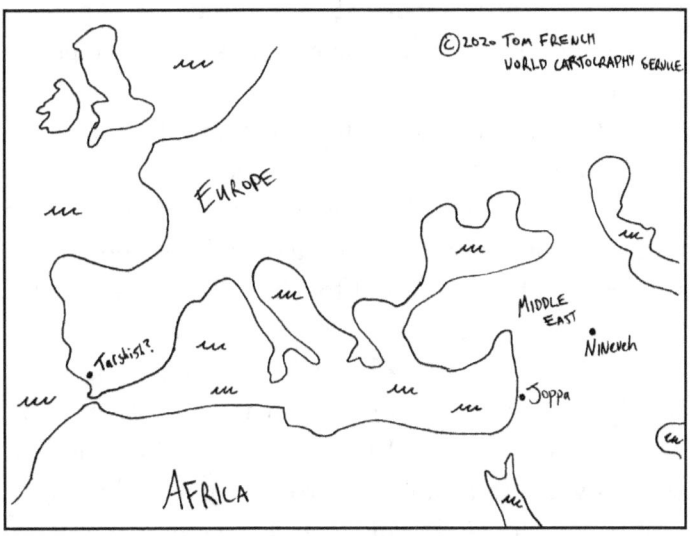

Tarshish is described in Isaiah 66:19 as a place where they had not heard of God's fame or seen his glory. To run to Tarshish was to go to a place where God was not.

The problem is, Jonah couldn't outrun God. If you have the sensitivity to know exactly where your crush is in a crowded room at all times, then getting on a boat isn't going to fool someone with all the tracking skills of the God of the universe. As if just to let Jonah know that he hadn't been fooled, God threw a storm at the boat.

The storm was so violent that the boat threatened to break up. What's interesting is that in the original Hebrew that this was written in, the word 'threatened' is a word used for people, not objects. It's as if the ship is thinking to itself, 'This sucks! I might just fall apart. That'd be much easier than carrying on.' When the weather is so bad that the ship is considering ending it all, you know it's a bad storm. The sailors responded with fear and were praying to any god. Meanwhile, Jonah was asleep, avoiding the real God.

God didn't send the storm to punish Jonah; he sent it to wake him up. Sometimes we need the trouble in our lives to let us know that we're going against the good design God has for us. Like when our selfish actions cause trouble for others, as it did for the sailors onboard with Jonah, or when the sin we thought would make us happy makes us feel dirty instead, or when our friends point out our flaws and we feel hurt and embarrassed. All of these, as hard as they are, can be gifts from God. Anytime your sin gets you into trouble, it's probably not God trying to destroy you. It's God trying to wake you up.

How do we know God isn't punishing us? Because when we look at Jesus, we can see what God's punishment really looks like. It's not just a hard time, it's the terrible, soul destroying, wrath of God we see poured out on Jesus at the cross. You and I don't need to experience that because of what Jesus went through for us. The storms of our sin are God waking us up so that we may see how far we have strayed from him.

SOMETHING TO REFLECT ON:
When have you experienced difficulties in your life because of your sin? Looking back, how can you see God using it to call you back to himself?

SOMETHING TO DO:
If you're in the midst of a storm right now of your own making, are you awake or asleep? How will you turn back to God?

A PRAYER TO PRAY:
Lord God, I know that my sin can cause trouble for me and others. Thank you for Jesus, and that you do not seek to destroy me, but to awaken me and draw me back to you.

DAY FOUR

Bad Reputation

FOCUS VERSES: JONAH 1:6–10

READ: Jonah 1:6–17

SOME THINGS TO CONSIDER:
I once woke up to find my boss standing in front of me, with his phone out, taking a photo of me while I slept. This would have been weird and creepy, except I had fallen asleep at my desk at work when I was meant to be, well, working. He was taking a photo because he thought it was funny, which was a much better outcome than getting fired.

    I can imagine when the captain found Jonah sleeping that he wouldn't have found it as funny as my boss. Everyone else was fighting and praying for their

Day Four: Bad Reputation

lives while Jonah was catching some shut-eye. On deck, the sailors had been praying to every god they could think of – Baal, Zeus, Thor, the god of pancakes, whoever! Not one of their prayers had worked, but maybe, the captain thinks, Jonah has a god he knows of but they don't. 'Get up and call on your god!' the captain yelled at him. What a rude awakening! Remember yesterday how we talked about God telling Jonah to get up? Now the captain was telling him to do the same thing. The command of God was on the lips of the pagan sailor.

When Jonah came up on deck, they cast lots to figure out who was responsible for the terrible storm they were facing. I like to think they played Scissors, Paper, Rock but I'm not sure that had been invented yet.[4]

When it became clear that Jonah was responsible, they bombarded him with questions. They wanted to know his job, where he lived, his country, and his people. These weren't just get-to-know-you questions; they believed that people groups and locations had their own specific gods, so if they could determine Jonah's god, they could figure out how to escape the storm. They needed to ask these questions because nothing from Jonah's behaviour made

---

4. My editor mentioned that the game is more commonly known as Rock, Paper, Scissors, which I disagreed with. This caused me to do an Instagram poll, to which 77 per cent of respondents voted for Scissors, Paper, Rock. The rest voted for Rock, Paper, Scissors, and a few anarchists messaged me to say the correct order is Paper, Rock, Scissors or some other nonsense. However, most of the people who voted for Scissors, Paper, Rock were from my home state of New South Wales, and most of the people who voted for something else were outside NSW, including a few in the UK where my editor resides. So, if you have been triggered by the incorrect order of words in naming this game, I sincerely apologise. You can send your complaints to hello@tomfrench.com.au, however I take no responsibility for any psychological harm done.

it clear that he was a worshipper of Yahweh, only that he was running from him. (Yahweh is the ancient name for our God, who was also the God of Jonah.) The sailors were becoming the collateral damage of Jonah's own broken relationship with God, and they wanted to put a stop to it before everyone drowned.

When Jonah responded to the sailor's questions, he didn't answer them all, but he did say, 'I worship the Lord, the God of heaven, who made the sea and the dry land' (1:9). Which only highlighted the stupidity of Jonah's desire to run from the God of the ocean on the ocean, but little of Jonah's behaviour makes sense or reflects that he truly loves and honours his God.

Would the people in your life know from the way you live that you are a follower of Jesus? Jesus calls us to be 'salt and light' in the world, people who make the world better, pointing them to the love and truth of God so that others 'may see your good deeds and glorify your Father in heaven' (Matthew 5:16). Jonah was living in the exact opposite way, and he was bringing calamity on these innocent sailors because of his disobedience.

Christians don't always get a good rap in the world. Sometimes it's because we're holding fast to God's word and living lives that honour him, which offends the people around us. But sometimes it's because we're holding onto prejudices and disguising them as religion, or we're imposing our morality on others who don't worship our God, when we should be introducing them to the God who loves them, and letting him be the one who judges and changes hearts.

Day Four: Bad Reputation

Other people shouldn't suffer because of the way we choose to live out our faith. Jesus was the most uncompromising follower of God, and he did not inflict suffering on those he encountered but brought healing and truth. In fact, instead of bringing suffering he took the suffering of the world upon himself at the cross, defeating sin and death and offering new life to all.

We should be known for being followers of the God of heaven and earth. Not because we bring storms and disaster upon those around us, but because, by living like Jesus, we bring love and truth to bear, even to the point of suffering for the sake of the world, like Jesus did for us.

Peter encouraged the readers of his letter to live the opposite way to Jonah, and he encourages us too: 'Live such good lives among the pagans that, though they accuse you of doing wrong, they may see your good deeds and glorify God on the day he visits us' (1 Peter 2:12).

SOMETHING TO REFLECT ON:
Who in your life reflects the love of Jesus, in their words and actions of truth and love? How have they shown you more of what God is like?

SOMETHING TO DO:
Find one thing you can do today to show the love of Jesus to those around you by your words and actions so that they may know God better.

A PRAYER TO PRAY:

God of heaven, I am sorry that I do not always live in a way that reflects your love to the world. Thank you that Jesus has shown us how to live in the world. Help me reflect his love and truth to all those around me.

DAY FIVE

The Goodness of Pagans

FOCUS VERSES: JONAH 1:11–16

READ: Jonah 1:6–17

SOME THINGS TO CONSIDER:

If someone gets an electric shock and their heart stops pumping properly, to save them they need an electric shock to get their heart back into its right rhythm. This seems like a strange solution. 'That person is dying! Quick, give then an electric shock!' But sometimes, novel problems require novel solutions.

As everyone faced drowning in the storm, Jonah had a solution. 'Pick me up and throw me into the sea!' he cried. This seems overly dramatic. At least for the first option.

'Perhaps we could try rowing and drop you off on the land?' one of the sailors may have piped up. So they tried that, but the storm grew worse. It's interesting that even those sailors, who were not believers, and who were in terrible danger because of Jonah's storm, were still keen to risk their lives to save their troublesome passenger rather than throw him overboard.

Faced with (they assume) killing Jonah, the sailors prayed to Yahweh. Jonah, the prophet, never prayed to his God, but the pagan sailors did. They didn't want to be held responsible for killing Jonah. He hadn't done them any wrong, and they wanted God to know that even though they were killing his prophet, this beef was between Jonah and him.

But, finally, they tossed Jonah into the sea, and everything became calm.

This reminds me of another story where a different man was sleeping in a boat. There was a big storm and he woke up and calmed it (Mark 4:35–41). It seems that in The Bible's Guide to Boating, if you get into a big storm, go find the person in your boat who's sleeping. If it's Jesus, ask him to calm the storm. If it's not, throw the sleeping person overboard, and that'll calm it too. But make absolutely sure that if you find Jesus asleep in your boat you don't throw him overboard as that would be extremely embarrassing.

Having seen the power of Yahweh, the sailors worshipped him. They made vows and sacrifices, and seeing as sacrifices required killing animals (which had probably been tossed into the sea by this point) and

Day Five: The Goodness of Pagans

burning the carcasses (very dangerous on a wooden ship), they would have had to go to land, find a temple for Yahweh in Israel, and do their worship there. This was not some short-lived change of heart; they were converted, their lives had changed. How amazing that God still uses Jonah in his sin to bring people to faith in him. This isn't an excuse to sin, but it can at least bring you comfort if you feel you're not very good at helping people meet Jesus. And whatever you're doing as you share your faith, you're not threatening the lives of a ship full of humans. At least I hope you're not.

The irony of this story is that the pagan sailors are better followers of Yahweh than Jonah, the supposed prophet, is. They pray to God when Jonah won't. They try to save Jonah when all he has done is bring them harm. They commit themselves to Yahweh while Jonah avoids his commitment even to the point of death.

I don't know if you are ever surprised by the sin of Christians, or the goodness of those people who aren't, but according to the story of Jonah, neither of these things should surprise us. It's not unusual for people who aren't Christians to lead better, more loving, more kind-hearted lives than many Christians. Sometimes, especially if you live in a Christian bubble, you can get the impression that everyone who is not a Christian is evil, or at very least, not that good. But an atheist stripper (for example) can act in ways that are kinder and more loving than a fourth-generation Christian pastor (for example).

Following Jesus doesn't make you morally superior to other people. It only makes you morally superior to your former self as the Holy Spirit works in you and grows his fruit in your life.

The only one who is truly superior is also the only one who can truly calm our greatest storm. No one is good enough to save themselves. Jonah saved the sailors from the consequences of his own sin by allowing himself to be thrown to his death. Jesus, the sinless one, saves us from the storm of God's wrath as he gives up his life, so we might live to worship him. From the worst behaved Christian to the best behaved pagan, this is good news for anyone who would put their trust in him.

SOMETHING TO REFLECT ON:
How have you assumed you are morally superior to the people around you? How has that stopped you from properly loving them?

SOMETHING TO DO:
Pay attention to the goodness you see in all people, no matter who they are, Christian or not, and take time to thank God for their actions.

A PRAYER TO PRAY:
Father God, all of us have sinned and fall short of your glory. All of us are in need of your mercy. Help me to trust in Jesus for my goodness as I seek to help others to trust in Jesus' goodness to save them.

DAY SIX

Fish Time

FOCUS VERSE: JONAH 1:17

READ: Jonah 1:6–17

SOME THINGS TO CONSIDER:
It's time to talk about the fish!

If you knew anything about the book of Jonah before these devotions, then you probably know that Jonah got swallowed by a fish, or perhaps a whale (the ancient writers didn't distinguish between fish and whales, so it could have been either). This is certainly the thing that is most exciting to talk to kids about. But, as great as the giant man-swallowing aquatic rescue creature is, it's not the point of the story. The fish only gets a mention in three of Jonah's forty-eight verses. But seeing as today we're looking at one of those verses, we can talk about the fish.

Do you think the fish existed? Don't be afraid to answer; no one will hear you, and you won't offend me either way.

Some people feel that it's very important that everyone believes in the fish because if you don't believe in the fish, which the Bible *very clearly teaches*, then you obviously don't believe what the Bible says is true, and then why would you trust in God? You're basically a truth-hating atheist!

I'm not sure it's as clear-cut as that. The book of Jonah may be an ancient 'alternative history' parable about the prophet Jonah, son of Ammitai. As a fictional account of a real person, it teaches readers about how they should view God's judgement, and relate to groups of people they don't like, rather than function as a record of something that actually happened.

Of course, the book of Jonah may be an entirely true story, and the fish might have really been an actual fish. It may be physically impossible for a human to survive inside a fish for three days and three nights, but then again the Bible is full of miraculous things that shouldn't happen, but I'm sure did happen. A man raising people from the dead, and then rising from the dead himself, to name just two examples. God can do any miracle he wants, and if he wanted to save Jonah, he would have. For all we know, perhaps God sent a time-travelling submarine with excellently appointed living quarters inside to pick Jonah up, which the ancient writers just classified as a fish.[5] For the record, I think that's the least likely of the options. I'm simply saying, God can do what he wants. The fish isn't the first miracle we've encountered in Jonah, and it won't be the last. A miracle is a miracle; that's what makes it a miracle.

Whether you think there was a fish or not I'll leave up to you, because, well, the point of the fish isn't the fish.[6]

So what is the point of the fish? The fish is a rescue fish. God sent the fish to save Jonah when he should have drowned. God could have easily let Jonah sink to the ocean floor to become fish food in the normal sense and found someone else to go preach to the Ninevites, but he didn't. Instead, he saved him in the belly of a giant, smelly marine redeemer to give him a second chance.

The great miracle is the miracle of God's grace. God is a god of second chances. Just as he could have left Jonah, he could leave all of us to receive the just desserts for our rebellion against him. We have all tried to run from his presence in different ways, and refused to do what he has called us to do, and yet – and yet! – he came himself on the most unlikely of rescue missions, to save not through a fish, but in a far messier, more unpleasant way – being executed, naked and bleeding on a cross, by the very people he was rescuing.

---

5. Maybe Jonah had a mate in the submarine, Australian Prime Minister Harold Holt. Feel free to look Mr Holt up on Wikipedia when the devotion is done if this footnote makes no sense to you.

6. If you really want to know what I think about the book of Jonah, and whether I believe it's a work of fiction or not, you can read about it in the Introduction. Or if you're one of those people who reads the Introduction, then you already know what I think.

There is a miracle you should get caught up on. It's that, if you trust in Jesus, you too have been rescued from death by the God of the universe who gave his life for you.

If you want to think about the fish, let it remind you that God has given you a second chance too. Live your life with the vigour and excitement of a person who has been miraculously saved from death.

SOMETHING TO REFLECT ON:
What is your rescue story? How did you come to trust in God's salvation for you in Jesus? And if you haven't yet, will you put your trust in Jesus?

SOMETHING TO DO:
Spend time today thanking God for his rescue of you through Jesus.

A PRAYER TO PRAY:
Gracious God, thank you that you work miracles every day as you forgive people and give them second chances through the saving work of Jesus. Help me to always be thankful for how you have rescued me.

DAY SEVEN

Rescue Song

FOCUS VERSES: JONAH 2:1–4

READ: Jonah 2

SOME THINGS TO CONSIDER:
Have you ever watched a musical and thought, 'Wouldn't it be great if we just broke out in song all the time?' Some of my favourite dreams have been when a song is playing as my alarm, and I've dreamt that the song is happening in my dream, and I feel like I'm in a literal music video.

As Jonah was inside the fish, he broke out in song. Or at the very least, he broke out in poetry. It may not be a rousing musical number with a killer dance routine, but give the guy a break, he is stuck in a marine animal.

What it is, is a heartfelt expression of thankfulness to God for saving him.

Of course, it may seem weird that Jonah was praising God for what he had done when he was stuck inside a fish. But remember Jonah was on his way to death. He was going to drown in the sea. For ancient Israelites like Jonah, the sea was a place of chaos and danger. When Jonah went into the water, he wasn't expecting to survive. And yet, God is in charge of even the places that seem most terrifying and chaotic. Nothing is beyond God's power, and so he sent a fish, the most unconventional lifesaving craft ever.

Responding to his fishy rescue, Jonah prayed. The prayer he prayed was mostly a collection of phrases taken from other prayers in the Bible, from the book of Psalms. This isn't because Jonah was some kind of prayer plagiariser. Rather, he'd grown up praying the Psalms with his family and community, and when he needed to pray, those prayers would have been right there, ready to express what he was feeling. I know that has happened to me; I have said something in a prayer which sounded beautiful, wise, and true, and before I got to congratulate myself for my great prayer skills, I realised the reason why it sounded so good was just because I was praying something I had read in the Bible. One of the advantages of knowing your Bible is that sometimes it helps you to know how to pray to God when you don't have the words yourself.

As you read Jonah's prayer, you'll notice that God is the principal mover in everything: God hurled

Day Seven: Rescue Song

Jonah into the deep, all God's waves swept over Jonah, and God saved Jonah. Then Jonah said, 'I have been banished from your sight' (2:4), which seems a bit rich, seeing as all Jonah's trouble came about not because God randomly banished him but because he was literally running away from God! Jonah was in a mess, but a mess of his own making, and still God was kind enough to save him.

Notice also that Jonah prayed, 'From deep in the realm of the dead I called for help' (2:2). Jonah didn't actually die, but he saw himself as good as dead. Jonah may not be self-aware, but he is at least God-aware, fully aware that he should be dead, and God in his kindness saved him.

The amazing thing that the Bible teaches us is that before we are saved, we are dead in our sin (Ephesians 2:1–2). And yet, God did not wait to hear our cry to rescue us: 'This is love: not that we loved God, but that he loved us and sent his Son as an atoning sacrifice for our sins' (1 John 4:10). Before we had even had a chance to begin our life of sin against God, he had mounted a rescue mission for us.

I know life can sometimes feel pretty rubbish, perhaps like you're stuck in the belly of a fish. But if God was willing to save you while knowing of all your sin, he hasn't given up on you now. Jonah looked forward to a time when he would see God's temple (Jonah 2:4), the place of his presence, but now, by the Holy Spirit, we have become God's temple – God dwells in us. You have not been, and never will be, abandoned. Cry out to God at anytime, and break into poetry or song about anything, because he is with you.

SOMETHING TO REFLECT ON:
If you could break out in song or poetry to God right now, what would your message to God be?

SOMETHING TO DO:
Spend time composing a prayer to God, expressing to him how you feel about what he has done for you. If you don't feel like you're in a place where you can praise God like Jonah, that's okay. Just tell him how you feel. He can take it.

A PRAYER TO PRAY:
God, sometimes life feels pretty tough, but I thank you that even in the most difficult times I can remember how you have saved me through Jesus. I know that whatever situation I am in will not last forever, but your love will never end.

DAY EIGHT

Prophet in a Foxhole

FOCUS VERSES: JONAH 2:5–7

READ: Jonah 2

SOME THINGS TO CONSIDER:
Have you ever heard the phrase 'There are no atheists in foxholes'? It doesn't mean that all foxes believe in God. Of course, that could be true, I just don't know many foxes, so it's hard for me to assess their faith. Foxholes, apart from being the place where foxes live, are also the small holes that soldiers dig to fire from and shelter from the enemy. The phrase means when you're in one of those holes, sheltering for your life, in danger of dying at any moment, whatever beliefs you may have had about

the non-existence of God go out the window as you cry out to him to save you.[7]

The question I have about Jonah's prayer is whether this is what was going on for him. Obviously, he wasn't an atheist. This is clear partly because there were far fewer atheists in ancient times, but also because if he were an atheist he wouldn't be running from a God he didn't believe existed. But was Jonah experiencing a near-death conversion? And if he was, does it matter?

Jonah thought he was going to die. Not only had he been accosted in the face by seaweed (2:5) (seaweed is gross at the best of times), but he had sunk to the 'roots of the mountains' (2:6), the place where the tall mountains meet the ocean floor. He had gone to the pit of death and the gates had been locked behind him (he's speaking metaphorically; there aren't actual gates as far as I know).

It was only when his life was ebbing away that he 'remembered' God. Only on the brink of death did he decide it was a good time to pray. If Jonah was a committed follower of God, he would have been praying the whole way through. What right does he even have to pray? If he ran away from God before, why does he think God will listen when he cries out now? But, despite Jonah's dubious motivation, his prayer rose to God's holy temple – that is, God heard him and responded.

Have you ever felt like you couldn't talk to God because you were in a mess of your own making? Perhaps

---

7. Apparently there was a study done by the National Bureau of Economic Research that found there are actually only 8.9 per cent fewer atheists in foxholes, which is interesting but not the point of my illustration. See https://www.nber.org/papers/w24954

you had been living in a way you knew God wouldn't be pleased with, so you didn't feel like your prayer would be appropriate or make any difference to God. I know when I have sinned against God, I often don't want to pray because I don't feel worthy of talking to him. Why should he listen to me?

But, fantastically, just as God listened to Jonah, we can call out to God at any time, in any situation, and he will listen to us and respond. He doesn't just listen to the obedient people, or the faithful people. He'll hear anyone's prayer. When Jesus was on the cross, we see this in action. As he was dying between two criminals, one of them mocked him, but the other defended Jesus:

> 'Don't you fear God,' he said, 'since you are under the same sentence? We are punished justly, for we are getting what our deeds deserve. But this man has done nothing wrong.' Then he said, 'Jesus, remember me when you come into your kingdom.' Jesus answered him, 'Truly I tell you, today you will be with me in paradise.' (Luke 23:40-43)

Jesus could easily have said to the man, 'Bit late for you, buddy, you should have thought about this earlier.' But even though the criminal was dying after a life of rebellion, it was not too late for his request to be heard or to find salvation.

I don't know where you're at with God or where you'll be in the future, but if you're feeling overwhelmed by circumstances of your own making, call out to God, even if you are at the gates of death – your prayers can rise to God's holy temple.

SOMETHING TO REFLECT ON:
When have you felt like God might not listen to your prayers? How does the story of Jonah change how you view those situations?

SOMETHING TO DO:
Next time you don't think you can talk to God, remember Jonah, and that God will always listen to your prayer.

A PRAYER TO PRAY:
Merciful God, thank you that you always hear my prayers, even if I do not feel worthy of speaking to you. Thank you that Jesus makes me worthy, and your Spirit intercedes for me, that my prayers may be heard.

DAY NINE

The Idolater

FOCUS VERSES: JONAH 2:8–9

READ: Jonah 2

SOME THINGS TO CONSIDER:
You've probably seen something like this play out: a celebrity gets called out for saying or doing something inappropriate, and in response they make a public apology, promising to be better, and vowing to give money to charity as a sign of their new-found understanding that what they did was wrong. I don't know about you, but I'm usually sceptical that the person really has changed. I assume that most of the time they are apologising because they were caught, or to stop the online abuse, rather than because they are truly repentant.

As we come to the end of Jonah's prayer, the fact may strike you that his prayer sounds very pious and repentant, maybe somewhat like an ancient version of the celebrity apology. Maybe it was real, or maybe he hadn't changed at all.

In the prayer Jonah proclaimed: 'Those who cling to worthless idols turn away from God's love for them' (2:8), and then promised: 'But I, with shouts of grateful praise, will sacrifice to you' (2:9). It's as if, from the belly of the fish, Jonah was throwing shade on the sailors who turned to their idols (that is, false gods) when they were in trouble. While they might miss out on God's love, Jonah was going to make sacrifices to God. He wouldn't miss out on God's love because he knew and worshipped the true God, unlike those pagan sailors. But Jonah didn't know what we know. The sailors who worked so hard to save Jonah also recognised the power of Yahweh, the true God, and made sacrifices to him. While Jonah was hanging out in the fish, they were faithfully embracing the love of God.

Of course, what Jonah said in his prayer is true. Those who turn to false gods do miss out on God's love for them. But Jonah was the one who turned to an idol. Perhaps he hadn't worshipped a lesser god like Baal, Ashtoreth, or Loki, but he had chosen his own desires over God. He had turned to the worthless idol of his own righteousness, committing the original sin of thinking he knew better than God. As a result, he was missing out on God's love. Jonah shouldn't have thought so highly of himself.

Jonah's attitude to the sailors here shows his attitude to anyone who wasn't a worshipper of Yahweh

Day Nine: The Idolater

like he was. We'll see more in the following days how Jonah had a rather prejudiced views of foreigners. Despite Jonah's contrition, he probably hadn't changed much.

Jonah finished the prayer by promising: 'What I have vowed I will make good. I will say, "Salvation comes from the Lord"' (2:9), which seems weird again. Because all that Jonah vowed, as far as we can tell, was to run from God's call. So either Jonah was rewriting history to pretend he was planning to be faithful all along, or he made a vow to God that we have not been privy to.

Whatever the case, God would take Jonah up on his vow. The story of Jonah doesn't end in the fish. Jonah may not have fully become the man that we would expect him to become – all his rough edges weren't shaved off, all his prejudiced views weren't fixed, and all his idols weren't yet smashed – but still, he was finally willing to obey God, and that was enough. God can do anything with a believer's obedient heart.

Perhaps that's something you need to hear today. You may look at yourself and realise that you still have so many things wrong with you, and that's not to mention the idols and prejudiced attitudes you haven't even recognised yet. But they don't disqualify you from God's love, nor from his desire to shape you and use you for his purposes.

At this point in the story, Jonah is not yet the man he should be, and at this point in your story, you're not yet the person you should be. 'While we were still sinners, Christ died for us,' it says in Romans 5:8. God's love and purposes for us are not dependent on us having changed or the genuineness of our public apologies. Salvation comes before obedience, and obedience comes amid change. (And if you're worried about how genuine your obedience is, you're in a better place than the person who assumes all their motives are good.)

So, don't wait till you've got it all together before you make good on your vows to God. Jesus has made the acceptable sacrifice of himself to God, and now with shouts of grateful praise you can live the life you've been called to, as you become more and more the person you were made to be.

SOMETHING TO REFLECT ON:
How have you seen God use you, even when your attitude has been wrong?

SOMETHING TO DO:
Ask God what he wants you to do today. When you know the answer, do it and pay attention to how God uses even you.

A PRAYER TO PRAY:
Gracious God, thank you that you love and use people like Jonah and like me, even with our prejudiced attitudes and wrong motives. Please change me to become more like your Son Jesus, full of genuine love for you and all people. And as you change me, please help me to be obedient, that I might see you work in perfect ways through imperfect me.

DAY TEN

Fish Vomit

FOCUS VERSE: JONAH 2:10

READ: Jonah 2

SOME THINGS TO CONSIDER:

Here's the thing. This verse may not need an entire day dedicated to it, but how often do you get the chance to spend a day reflecting on biblical vomit? May Jonah 2:10 be a verse of life for you today![8]

Remember how Jonah's unfaithfulness is continually contrasted with the faithfulness of others? The sailors pledged faithfulness to Yahweh. God commanded a storm, and it did exactly what it was

---

8. Want more biblical vomit? More classic biblical spew can be found in Proverbs 26:11 and Isaiah 28:7–8. Feel free to bring them up with your pastor (pun intended).

told. And now we read about a faithful fish, who had been ordained by God to swallow Jonah, obeying God's command to vomit him back up.

Of course, this might have been exactly what the fish wanted to do. I assume having Jonah inside it wasn't all that comfortable. Which I guess shows just one more way the fish was a better follower of Yahweh than Jonah: swallowing a human may have felt as uncomfortable to the fish as preaching to Nineveh was a discomfort to Jonah, but the fish just got on and did it. Finally, three days later, the fish was able to have a good spew, and I'm sure it felt a lot better after that thunder chunder. When you're feeling gross, sometimes there's nothing better than a good vom. Things improved for the fish, and now the seaside ralphing gave Jonah the second chance he needed to return to doing the will of God.

I suspect that, while probably few of us have experienced being swallowed and spewed by God's oceanic servant, there may have been people in your life who have played a similar role for you. People who have taken on the unpleasant task of calling you on your sin and calling you back to faithfulness. It's not always a fun job, because no one wants to be told they're disobeying God. Spare a thought for them, whether they're parents, friends, youth leaders, pastors, teachers, coaches, or someone else – having those conversations is hard. But when they come, when you realise God is using someone else's faithfulness to call you back to obedience, take the time to listen. It can be tempting to take offence, and to immediately defend yourself, but remember that having

Day Ten: Fish Vomit

hard conversations is probably about as fun for them as it is for you.

Of course, there are people who take pleasure in telling others off. They lash out at others' sin, or they make up sin in an attempt to control others, and in the process sin themselves. But the people I'm talking about here are those who take the time to call out your sin gently, so they can invite you back into faithfulness with God. They are doing the work of the faithful fish, so be wise about how you respond to them, and don't attack them for helping you return to God's will. Something we can say for Jonah is that at least he didn't turn around and punch the fish in its nose as soon as he was out of its gullet.

So what should you do? Listen carefully to what they have to say, thank them for having the courage to bring this up with you, then take it to God, asking him to show you where their words might be true, so that you may return to the path of obedience.

Now that we're at the final paragraph for today, you may be feeling like I stretched the point. It was just a fish with a bellyache. But at least consider this: God has used greater things than a fish to bring us to faithfulness. He himself came to die and rise again to bring us to righteousness, and now he lives with us by the Holy Spirit, convicting us of our sin and changing us to be more like Jesus. God will move heaven and earth to bring us back to him. Maybe as he does you'll encounter a fish, foe, or friend; definitely you'll meet a Father, Son, and Holy Spirit. When you find, one more time, that God is calling you back to him, thank him that he spares nothing on our behalf, not a fish, and not a Son, and return to obeying God. It'll be a lot easier than getting swallowed and spewed by obedient marine life.

SOMETHING TO REFLECT ON:
How do you respond when people confront you with your sin? Are there ways you can respond better when people take the time to have hard conversations with you?

SOMETHING TO DO:
Remember someone who has lovingly called you out on your sin. Take the time to thank them for having the faithfulness and courage to call you back to obedience.

A PRAYER TO PRAY:
God of all creation, thank you that you moved heaven and earth to make me righteous by your Son. Help me to respond with faithfulness when you call me back to obedience. Thank you for all the people who help me love and obey you better.

DAY ELEVEN

Words of Power

FOCUS VERSES: JONAH 3:1–5

READ: Jonah 3

SOME THINGS TO CONSIDER:

Yesterday when we left Jonah, he had been vomited out by his rescuer fish. Today we pick up reading how God gave Jonah a renewed call to do what he'd asked him to do before. Notice how God didn't rub it in – 'Now, Jonah, are you ready to do what I have already asked you to do?' God gave Jonah a second chance, and he didn't even make Jonah feel bad. God's good like that.

Jonah arrived in Nineveh, 'a very large city', which 'took three days to go through it' (3:3). Scholars have spent a lot of time discussing why the passage says this when it was possible to walk around ancient Nineveh in a few hours. I think the author might have used a bit of exaggeration to convey how big the city was. Like if I were to say, 'I went to New York and the buildings were so tall they were a danger to passing space stations.' You wouldn't think the ISS might accidentally run into the spire of the Empire State Building if they weren't careful; you would understand that I meant that the buildings were very tall. Nineveh, the writer was saying, was a very significant ancient city.

Imagine, then, being Jonah and having to preach against this giant city (by ancient standards) and its people who hate you. Remember how evil these people were? (If you can't, go back and have a quick look at Day Two.) It would be like going to preach God's judgement to a terrorist training camp full of thousands of angry terrorists. That would literally be terrifying.

But, after God's fishy acts of persuasion, Jonah finally did what he'd been asked to do. Well, at least, he did the bare minimum. He said, 'Forty more days and Nineveh will be overthrown' (3:4). It's an eight-word sermon (five words in the original Hebrew). Technically, he did what God asked of him, but he certainly didn't go overboard. He didn't tell the Ninevites what they had done wrong, what they should do to escape the overthrowing, or who would overthrow them.

Still, Jonah's grudging sermon turned out to be some of the most powerful preaching in history. We're told that 'The Ninevites believed God. A fast was proclaimed, and all of them, from the greatest to the least, put on sackcloth'

Day Eleven: Words of Power

(3:5). Notice they didn't believe Jonah; they believed God. Jonah may have done the laziest preaching in history, but as soon as they heard God's words from his mouth they were overthrown, not by fire and brimstone falling from heaven to destroy their city, but by the need to repent to God of their evil ways. Notice also how quick they were to respond; they didn't need a second call from God, they heard and obeyed immediately. Once again, the pagans showed up the prophet.

When Jonah spoke, the Ninevites heard God. When you listen to preaching, do you expect to hear God? It's easy to feel like Bible talks are going to be the dull part of church or youth group. But God can speak powerfully when people preach his words, even when they do a poor job like Jonah. Just as God speaks through the Bible, as people preach from the Bible they preach the word of God. That's powerful! God can overturn your entire life if you're expecting to hear from him.

If God speaks through preaching, then not only can he change your life, he can change the life of your friends and family, even your enemies. The Ninevites seemed like the most wicked people on the face of the earth, and yet the power of God's word was able to break through and turn them from evil to repentance. God can change even the most hardened people. Are you prepared to share God's word with them? You probably shouldn't preach eight sullen words in your town square like Jonah, but perhaps you can lovingly share with others the good news of God who has lived with us, as one of us, defeated sin and death, and now calls us to repentance and to follow him. It can feel like a foolish message, but it's the word of God that saves us from judgement, changes lives, and overthrows rebellious hearts.

SOMETHING TO REFLECT ON:
What is your attitude to God's word? Are you expectant of its power in your life and the life of others?

SOMETHING TO DO:
Who needs to hear God's word in your life? Don't be afraid to speak confidently today of what God has done for us all in his Son Jesus.

A PRAYER TO PRAY:
God who speaks, thank you that I have been changed by your word. Forgive me that I often underestimate its power. May I see you work powerfully to bring me and those around me to continued repentance and trust in you through your word.

DAY TWELVE

Hear, Feel, Do

FOCUS VERSES: JONAH 3:6-10

READ: Jonah 3

SOME THINGS TO CONSIDER:
We Christians love a good repentance story. When I was in youth group, there would often be a moment when someone would share their testimony about how they used to sell drugs and get in trouble with the police, but then they met Jesus and now they don't do it anymore. I'm not sure how many people really kept following Jesus, but those stories sure were impressive.

Imagine having the King of Nineveh share at youth group. What a great repentance story: 'I used to capture and torture people. I would murder my enemies in front of their families. But then I heard about God's judgement, and now I'm a changed man!' That would definitely be all anyone went home talking about that night.

It seems pretty impressive that despite Jonah's bare-minimum, eight-word sermon, his words reached the ears of the wicked king who, as soon as he heard it, commanded everyone, including the animals, to repent. I'm not sure a cow can repent of its evil ways and violence, but if any cow could it was a Ninevite cow.

The question is, did the city truly repentant? There is no indication that Nineveh stayed changed forever. But what we know is that their repentance was enough that God relented and chose not to bring the destruction he had threatened. This is not because God is like a wishy-washy substitute teacher who makes threats and never manages to follow through. Instead, when God warns of judgement it's not because he wants to see people destroyed but because he wants them to come to repentance (2 Peter 3:9). In fact, we know God does follow through, because he was so serious about sin that he dealt with it by bringing the judgement for sin on Jesus. God can forgive us and relent from punishment because 'God made him who had no sin to be sin for us, so that in him we might become the righteousness of God' (2 Corinthians 5:21).

What, then, does true repentance look like? The Ninevites heard God's word, felt the conviction to change, and then changed how they lived. That's what true repentance is: hear, feel, and do. Too often we hear God's word, feel convicted, and then go right back to living how we lived before. The measure of whether you have really repented of your sin is not how sad you feel about what you've done, but whether you are working with the Holy Spirit to live differently.

Sometimes the most impressive repentance stories come from the people with the most 'wicked' past, like selling drugs or terrorising neighbouring nations. This is because those sins can be easier to identify and turn from than much more 'acceptable' sins that even our Christian culture can turn a blind eye to, sins like greed, gossip, anger, apathy, idolising success and hard work, or inaction in the face of injustice, to name just a few.

Is there sin in your life that God is calling you to repent of? Can you recall times of feeling conviction from God that you didn't follow through on? What has God's word said to you today? What are you feeling? What do you need to do?

If you have already put your trust in Jesus, then God has relented from bringing his judgement upon you, not just for a time, but for eternity. Now it's time to live the life of repentance Jesus calls you to, one by one turning your back on the sins he makes known to you. Hear, feel, do.

Whatever your sin, may your testimony be the story of a life saved and changed by God, who rescued you from the destruction he has threatened.

SOMETHING TO REFLECT ON:
What 'acceptable' sins has God identified in your life? How might he be calling you to repent of them?

Jonah

SOMETHING TO DO:

Chances are, if you've heard God's word, and felt his conviction, you know what to do. Now is the time to do it.

A PRAYER TO PRAY:

Gracious God, thank you that because of Jesus we can be rescued from the destruction you have threatened. May I live a life of even greater repentance than the cows of Nineveh. Help me to hear your word, feel its weight, and do what it calls me to do.

DAY THIRTEEN

Family Values

FOCUS VERSES: JONAH 4:1-4

READ: Jonah 4

SOME THINGS TO CONSIDER:
Imagine being in Jonah's position. You have just preached the most successful sermon of your life. Thousands of people have responded and turned their lives around as a result. How are you going to feel? The logical response, you would think, is to be overjoyed. However, that's not how Jonah actually felt. Instead, he was angry. Why was Jonah angry at his success? For the second time in this story, we see Jonah pray. And what he prayed was much less eloquent and beautiful than his first prayer in chapter 2 (although it was perhaps more honest). He

prayed and told God that he was angry because he knew God would have compassion on the people of Nineveh because that's exactly what God is like.

Plot twist! We assumed that Jonah was running away from Nineveh because he was afraid that they'd skin him alive and microwave his eyeballs. While this may have been a legitimate fear, it wasn't the reason Jonah was running away. He was afraid that he would preach, the Ninevites would repent, and God wouldn't destroy them. Jonah hated the Ninevites so much, he didn't want to do anything that might help them escape God's judgement. Unfortunately for Jonah, his worst fears came true: God forgave!

When Jonah mentioned that God is 'gracious and compassionate… slow to anger and abounding in love' (4:2), he was quoting the Bible. In Exodus 34 God had told Moses to go up on a mountain and that he would cause all his glory to pass by. As he did so, he declared his name to Moses:

> 'The Lord, the Lord, the compassionate and gracious God, slow to anger, abounding in love and faithfulness, maintaining love to thousands, and forgiving wickedness, rebellion and sin. Yet he does not leave the guilty unpunished; he punishes the children and their children for the sin of the parents to the third and fourth generation.' (Exodus 34:6-7)

Day Thirteen: Family Values

Jonah thought that this promise to Moses was how God should behave only towards Israelites like Jonah. But God was behaving with compassion and grace towards all people. Jonah was angry at God for being exactly who he promised to be, and he was angry enough to die (4:3)! Getting angry at God for being compassionate is like getting angry at water for being wet. But Jonah hated the Ninevites so much he hoped that by running away from God, there would be no one to share the news of God's impending judgement, and God would destroy them. Perhaps that was why his sermon was so lacking. He hoped that he'd do a bad enough job that no one would change. I can imagine that even if he had tried preaching his sermon by whispering it to a wall in a back alley, still God would have got it done.

We may laugh at Jonah's absurd reaction, but don't miss the point. It's not beyond us to harbour hatred in our hearts towards other people or people groups, believing that they deserve all the evil that comes to them but we deserve God's love and kindness. Who would you love to see punished by God? The person who has been bullying you at school, or could it be someone who has been telling lies about you online? Maybe it's not a particular person, but a group, like racists and rapists, or perhaps people of a particular country, religion, or political persuasion? We live in an increasingly polarised time, where the people we don't like or who don't agree with us are not just different, but we believe them to be stupid, evil, or subhuman, worthy of having their lives ruined.

The truth is, none of us deserve God's forgiveness, and yet because of Jesus, grace and forgiveness is available to all people, even the people you disagree with, are afraid of, or hate. To decide that some people don't deserve God's love is to decide that you do deserve it. You're saying that you have done something worthy of God's forgiveness, when the Bible is clear that all of us deserve judgement and yet we can receive mercy because of God's character, not ours.

Now, as children of God, he invites us to take on the family values: grace and compassion. If they are what brought you into God's family, they are how we live now that we are part of God's family, even to those who are outside the family.

One final thing to notice is how God responds to Jonah. God would have been entirely within his rights to blast Jonah for his absurdity. Instead he gently asks him a question: 'Is it right for you to be angry? (4:4)' Perhaps that's a question God is asking you. As you evaluate your heart, and the people you have profound problems with, the people you would like to see destroyed, maybe it's time to ask God to help you let go of your right to be angry and take up the family values of our heavenly Father: compassion and grace, being slow to anger, and abounding in love and faithfulness.

SOMETHING TO REFLECT ON:
Which people or people groups are you harbouring anger towards in your heart?

Day Thirteen: Family Values

SOMETHING TO DO:
It can be really hard to let go of anger, hatred, and fear. Ask God to continue changing your heart so that yours may become like his.

A PRAYER TO PRAY:
God of compassion and grace, if anyone is right to be angry, it is you, yet because of the work of Jesus, you have let go of your anger and forgiven us. Help me become more like you, letting go of my right to be angry, so I may love like you.

DAY FOURTEEN

Ordered Love

FOCUS VERSES: JONAH 4:5–9

READ: Jonah 4

SOME THINGS TO CONSIDER:
Do you ever get overly invested in something that probably really doesn't deserve the amount of emotional energy you give it? My current kick is watching reality TV cooking shows. I seem to care a lot about the contestants and how well their dishes turn out. I really shouldn't care if a mum from Adelaide beats the odds and makes a yummy lemon tart, but for some reason I just don't want her to fail.

In today's reading, we see Jonah getting overly invested in a plant. After not responding to God's question in verse 4, Jonah stormed off to the east of Nineveh

Day Fourteen: Ordered Love

to watch the city in the vain hope that God might still destroy it. I've spent a lot of time sitting in the scorching sun looking over Sydney Harbour waiting to see the New Year's Eve fireworks. This is Jonah's much more morbid and vengeful fireworks vantage point.

As he sat in his makeshift shelter, God appointed a plant, in the same way he appointed the fish to swallow Jonah, to grow up over him. Jonah loved this plant. For the first time in the entire book of Jonah, he was 'very happy' (4:6). He wasn't 'very happy' about being saved from death by a fish, nor was he 'very happy' about his powerful sermon saving thousands of people from God's wrath. But then he got a plant to save him from some sunshine, and suddenly he was very happy.

Unfortunately, God appointed a worm (like the fish and the plant) to eat the plant, which withered and died, leaving the sun to beat down on Jonah's (probably) bald head. Then God appointed a scorching wind (like the fish, plant, and worm) just to top off Jonah's misery. How miserable was he? He was miserable enough to die!

God asked Jonah if it was right for him to be angry about the plant, and probably without thinking, Jonah came out with this absurd reply: 'It is... And I'm so angry I wish I were dead' (4:9). Come on, Jonah! Maybe keep your mouth shut for once. Couldn't he see that God was trying to teach him a lesson?

We're going to spend a bit of time looking at God's response to Jonah tomorrow, but it's clear that Jonah had some disordered loves. He was more invested in a plant than anything or anyone else in the story. When we love something more than we should, that's when things go bad. For instance, when we love being in a relationship more than we care for the person we're in relationship with, that's when things get toxic. When we love winning more than we care for the people we're playing with or against, that's when a game can lead us into sin. When we love getting good marks more than we care about loving the people we live and go to school with, that's when academic success has become an idol. There are a lot more examples – maybe you have some from your own life that are coming to mind.

Jesus summed up what the order of our loves should be when he taught that the two great commandments are loving God and loving others (Matthew 22:34–40). Anything that gets in the way of those two loves is a disordered love, like loving a plant more than you love seeing God have mercy. Jesus showed us what ordered love looks like when he loved God and us more than his own life and gave it up so that we might receive eternal life.

It's easy to get so invested in the things we enjoy, or the goals we have, that we allow them to lead us into sin. And yet, we can use the things we're invested in to help us love God and love others better! Imagine if Jonah invited some weary traveller to share his plant's shade with him (assuming there was a lonely traveller), then the thing he loved could help him love others. I love watching the reality TV cooking shows with my wife. It's a way that we spend time together, and the TV chefs inspire a love of food in me. Being in a romantic

Day Fourteen: Ordered Love

relationship can be a great opportunity to serve and care for someone. Playing games can help you enjoy and encourage your teammates and opponents. Academic success can honour God and allow you to better enjoy his world while using your knowledge and skills to serve others. The things we love too much are rarely bad they just take the wrong position in our lives. As you consider the things you love, ask God to show you if they are disordered, and how you could use them to better love him and others.

SOMETHING TO REFLECT ON:
What things do you love more than you should? How can you reorder it to help you love God and others more?

SOMETHING TO DO:
Choose one thing you have identified that may be a disordered love. Take an opportunity today to use it to love God or love others better.

A PRAYER TO PRAY:
Loving God, thank you that Jesus loved you and us more than he loved his own life. Please show me where I have loved things more than I have loved you or others. Please help me reorder my loves.

DAY FIFTEEN

The Last Question

FOCUS VERSES: JONAH 4:10–11

READ: Jonah 4

SOME THINGS TO CONSIDER:
So we come today to the end of the book of Jonah, and it ends, rather unexpectedly, with God asking Jonah another question. And strangely, we never hear his response.

Jonah had just told God that he was angry enough to die due to the loss of his plant. God seemed to think Jonah needed to gain a bit of perspective. Jonah did nothing to tend or grow the plant he was so fond of, yet he loved the plant. God created the people of Nineveh; shouldn't Jonah have accepted God's concern for them?

Day Fifteen: The Last Question

We also read that the people of Nineveh could not 'tell their right hand from their left' (4:11). This wasn't because they literally could not distinguish between left and right, as is often the case for me.[9] What it seems to mean is that the Ninevites were somewhat morally ignorant. They knew right and wrong, because God expected them to repent, and they were quick to recognise their evil in response to Jonah's preaching, but they didn't have God's law like Jonah did. They didn't have the same privileges of access to the word of God that Jonah had. Their ignorance was not a reason to judge them but to have compassion on them.

To top it all off, there were all those animals in the city, who probably hadn't committed a single war crime but would still suffer if God was to destroy the city. If Jonah cared about his plant, shouldn't God be concerned for those people and those animals?

So what of the question that we never read Jonah's answer to? This is probably for the best, because he most likely would have just said something dumb. What this does is force us to consider our own sense of compassion for God's creation, even those people who we might regard as enemies.

This was no hypothetical question for the readers of Jonah. Depending on when the book was written, Israel would either soon be invaded by the Assyrians (Nineveh was the capital of Assyria) or had already been conquered by them. Would the people of Israel

---

9. When I need to figure out left and right, I spend a lot of time looking at my hands to see which one can make an uppercase L with my thumb and index finger.

be willing to view even their worst enemies from the viewpoint of God? Would they be willing to accept God's compassion only for themselves, or would they accept that God's loving character applied to all people?

That doesn't mean God's judgement would never come – there was a time when the Assyrians were overthrown and Nineveh was destroyed. What it means is that Jonah, Israel, and also you and I, must entrust even our enemies to God, and allow him to do with them what he will. Jonah was never going to be able to bring destruction upon Nineveh by his running, his preaching, or anything else that was always God's prerogative. Jonah, however, was being asked to have the same heart for Nineveh that God had.

Perhaps these are the questions we all need to wrestle with. Do we have God's heart of compassion on all people? Are we willing to work for the good and salvation of even our worst enemies?

We can still long for God's justice to come. We know that the world's justice is inadequate and often as broken as the sin it responds to. We need to entrust all people, our friends, our foes, and everyone in between, to the perfect justice and mercy of God. So while God can worry about the big stuff, we concern ourselves with caring for even our enemies.

When we put our trust in Jesus, we become people who, despite our willing participation in evil, are loved and saved from God's judgement and adopted into his family. Jesus did not come to earth to preach an eight-word sermon and leave us to figure out the rest. And he did not just have concern for us from afar. Instead, he took on our concerns by becoming one of us. He came to preach repentance and belief, a turning back to God, knowing that it would cost him his life, as the people he came to save did not heed his words but killed him for them. He entirely invested himself in the work of our salvation.

The challenge for us to is to recognise that we are both the Ninevites and Jonah. We have received mercy and now we are being asked to show God's mercy. What would you rather? To be the angry fool on the hill, hoping for the destruction of your enemies, or to join God in his concern for the world, sharing the good news of his salvation, and getting to see lives graciously overthrown in the process?

SOMETHING TO REFLECT ON:
Who could God be showing you his concern for? How is he inviting you to share his love with them?

SOMETHING TO DO:
Keep your eye out today for the people you come across. Remind yourself as you see them that these are people loved by God. Remind yourself that you get to love them too.

A PRAYER TO PRAY:
God who is concerned for all, give me a heart of concern for all, even my enemies, so I may share with all people your love in the truth I speak and the things I do.

Afterword

Now that you've spent two weeks with Jonah, how do you feel about the guy? Do you like him? Do you pity him? Do you think he's a bit of a nong? My mother read these devotions and mentioned that I've been pretty harsh on Jonah. I assume this is because I identify with him, and I'm harsh on myself. I'm usually not the first person to give myself a break. Maybe you feel the same about yourself.

So, before I let you head off on your merry way, if you're feeling a little deflated as someone who has recognised Jonah-like tendencies in yourself, let me encourage you. A lot of people find similarities between the story of Jonah and the story Jesus told about the Prodigal Son (Luke 15:11–32). That's the story about a guy who took his inheritance early, left his father for dead, and lived it up. Everything was good till his money ran out, and he was forced to take a job feeding pigs just to stay alive. There, in the muck of the pig pen, hungry for the pigs' food, like Jonah in the belly of the

Afterword

fish, he came to his senses and decided to go back to his father and beg to be welcomed back into his household as a servant.

If you've heard the story before, you know what happens next. His father didn't make him grovel for a job; he welcomed him like his long-lost son (which he was), despite the fact that he'd treated his father so badly. The father threw a party and celebrated the return of his lost son.

We don't know what was going on in heaven when Jonah decided to return to the path that God had called him to, but I suspect there was a celebration or two up there. Even if our repentance, like Jonah's, isn't as all-encompassing as we would like, God doesn't need us to have everything perfectly in order before he can use us.

As you recognise your sin and choose to return to the path of obedience, do you know how God responds? With a party! Jesus said, 'I tell you that in the same way there will be more rejoicing in heaven over one sinner who repents than over ninety-nine righteous people who do not need to repent' (Luke 15:7). If you've seen something of yourself in Jonah and, with God's help, you're working to change how you live, then you can be sure that God is celebrating you. He's not sitting in heaven waiting for you to become perfect, he's rejoicing over you, even if you happen to get it wrong sometimes.

You may also remember that there was a second son in the story Jesus told – the older brother. That brother became angry when he found out about his father's extravagant party for his brother when he, who had never abandoned his father, didn't even get so much as a baby goat for his good behaviour.

In this son, you may see a different reflection of Jonah, as he was sitting on the hill waiting to see the wicked destroyed and feeling angry that God would show mercy to the people of Nineveh. Just as God talked with Jonah about his reasons for his compassion, the father in Jesus' story gives him an explanation for his extravagant grace:

> 'My son,' the father said, 'you are always with me, and everything I have is yours. But we had to celebrate and be glad, because this brother of yours was dead and is alive again; he was lost and is found.' (Luke 15:31-32)

For those of us who have seen our Jonah-like tendencies in our begrudging response to God's kindness to others, we have a message from God for us here too: we are his kids, we're always with him, and everything he has is ours! What an amazing message to get from God in the midst of our grumbling and stinginess. You may want to beat yourself up for your lack of grace towards your enemies, but God doesn't. No, he just wants you to know how much he loves you so that you may also be able to celebrate how much he loves others too.

Jonah doesn't come out looking so good at the end of the book, but when we look at his story in the big picture of what God is up to in the Bible, we can see that he's not a hopeless villain, but a bumbling, grumpy, very loved, child of God. Jesus' saving work on your behalf is clear evidence that you are deep in God's good graces – you don't die for someone you feel lukewarm about.

So as you consider the Ninevites in your life and take on the challenge of Jonah to align your heart with God's, remember God's heart towards you. You are loved, you are a child of God, he is always with you, and everything he has is yours. When you know you're loved, you'll know how to love.

Get the latest Pop's Devotions in your inbox:

tomfrench.com.au/devotions

Bibliography

Writing these devotions has taken a lot of help from wise people and Bible scholars. Throughout my life as a Christian, I have learnt about Jonah many times over, so I don't know where all my ideas have come from, but here are the major books (and one sermon series) I used to help me write these devotions. You wouldn't go too far wrong to look them up if you wanted to know more about the book of Jonah.

BOOKS

Leslie C. Allen, *The Books of Joel, Obadiah, Jonah, and Micah*. Grand Rapids: Eerdmans, 1976.

David W. Baker, T. Desmond Alexander and Bruce K. Waltke, *Obadiah, Jonah and Micah: An Introduction and Commentary*. Downers Grove: Inter-Varsity Press, 1988.

Mark E. Biddle, *A Time to Laugh: Humor in the Bible*. Macon: Smyth and Helwys, 2013.

James Bruckner, *The NIV Application Commentary: Jonah, Nahum, Habakkuk, Zephaniah*. Grand Rapids: Zondervan, 2004.

Sinclair B. Ferguson, *Man Overboard!: The Story of Jonah*. Edinburgh: Banner of Truth, 2008.

Timothy Keller, *The Prodigal Prophet: Jonah and the Mystery of God's Mercy*. London: Hodder & Stoughton, 2018.

Henry M. Morris, *The Remarkable Journey of Jonah: A Scholarly, Conservative Study of His Amazing Record*. Green Forest: Master Books, 2003.

Rosemary Nixon, *The Message of Jonah: Presence in the Storm*. Leicester: Inter-Varsity Press, 2003.

Billy K. Smith and Frank S. Page, *Amos, Obadiah, Jonah*. Nashville: Broadman & Holman, 1995.

Douglas Stuart, *Hosea–Jonah (World Biblical Commentary)*. Nashville: Thomas Nelson, 1987.

AND THAT ONE SERMON SERIES
Tim Mackie, 'The Amazing Jonah' Parts 1–5, *Exploring My Strange Bible* (podcast). https://bibleproject.com/podcast/series/the-amazing-jonah/

Also by Tom French

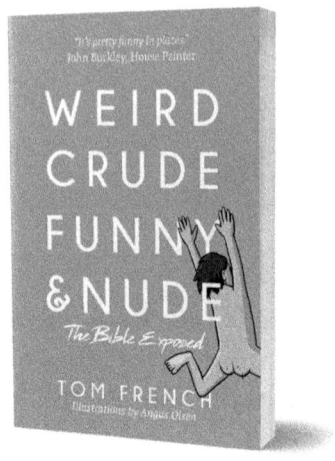

'Grab this book with both hands and see where it takes you!'
Ali Martin, Soul Survivor UK

Ultimate fighting bears, a fat king who poops himself, zombies, donkey 'bits', and a fart.

These are not the things you'd expect to find in the Bible, but they're all there. If you thought the Bible was dull, think again. This is your chance to discover all the parts of the Bible they don't teach you in Sunday school – but probably should.

Weird, Crude, Funny, and Nude is a hilarious, Christ-centred, and somewhat inappropriate look at some of the least known and discussed parts of the Bible – perfect for teenagers or any of us who think nudity, poop, and farts are funny.

Buy now at tomfrench.com.au

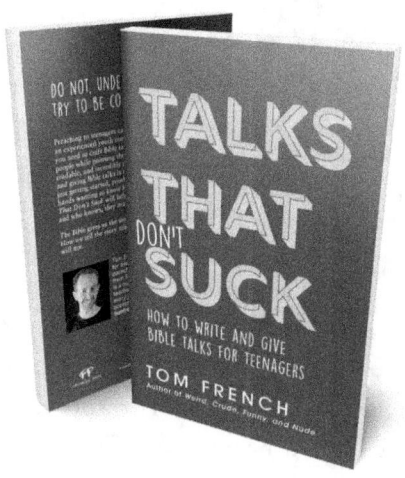

'Do not, under any circumstances, try to be cooler than you are.'

Preaching to teenagers can be a terrifying prospect. Tom French, an experienced youth communicator, will give you everything you need to craft Bible talks that engage and challenge young people while pointing them to the love of God in Jesus. This fun, readable, and incredibly practical step-by-step guide for writing and giving Bible talks is the ideal book for new youth leaders just getting started, youth pastors looking for a refresher, or old hands wanting to know how to speak to young people. *Talks That Don't Suck* will help you ensure your talks aren't terrible –and who knows, they may even be amazing!

The Bible gives us the story for all people, for all generations. How we tell the story might change, but the truth of the story will not.

Buy now at tomfrench.com.au

About the Author

Tom French is married to his excellent wife, Emily Sandrussi. He is also a youth ministry veteran, having spent the past two decades working with teenagers in churches and schools around Australia. Every year he teaches the Bible to thousands of young people in youth groups, churches, schools, and camps around the country. He has a Bachelor of Theology from Sydney Missionary and Bible College. Tom lives in Melbourne with Emily and his daughter, Layla. You can often find him at the movies eating popcorn for dinner.

Visit **tomfrench.com.au** to sign up for blog updates and the latest on new books. There you can also listen to Tom's sermons, book Tom to speak, see a photo of Tom holding a microphone, and much more.

YouTube: **youtube.com/twfrench**
Instagram: **@twfrench**
Facebook: **facebook.com/twfrench**

Podcast: Search for '**Tom French Preaching**' in your favourite podcast app.